Carroll Davidson Wright

The Relation of Political Economy to the Labor Questions

Carroll Davidson Wright

The Relation of Political Economy to the Labor Questions

ISBN/EAN: 9783337077716

Printed in Europe, USA, Canada, Australia, Japan

Cover: Foto ©Suzi / pixelio.de

More available books at **www.hansebooks.com**

THE RELATION

OF

POLITICAL ECONOMY

TO

THE LABOR QUESTION.

BY

CARROLL D. WRIGHT,

CHIEF OF THE MASS. BUREAU OF STATISTICS OF LABOR,
ETC., ETC.

BOSTON:
A. WILLIAMS AND COMPANY.
1882.

THE following Essay constituted the first of a course of lectures upon "Phases of the Labor Question Ethically considered," which were delivered before the Lowell Institute in December, 1879. I have used some of the thoughts, and expressions even, of this lecture in other works and upon other occasions since it was first delivered ; but it is now given in full as it was delivered.

This lecture is published to meet the wishes of those who have kindly remembered it ; and it is dedicated to "sober, industrious, and thrifty workingmen, and humane, large-hearted employers, . . . two types of men I prefer to speak to."

C. D. W.

READING, MASS., May, 1882.

THE RELATION OF POLITICAL ECONOMY TO THE LABOR QUESTION.

I SHALL speak to you of the demands labor is making or will make upon political economy.

The labor question, a short term for the evolution of industrial forces, includes a wide range of sociological studies, a general treatment of which would be impossible. I shall not, therefore, undertake to discuss the labor question in its comprehensiveness, but only a phase of it. You must not, however, consider the matters I do not touch to be held in my own estimation as unimportant. I simply treat a side I have considered to some extent, fully recognizing the paramount importance of those features I cannot mention even.

I shall constantly use the term "labor question" as

embracing the wants of the wage-laborer, or in a general way as representing the discussion of the just and equitable distribution of profits, or the products of labor and capital. In this are to be found the vital elements of the labor question, whether from an economical or an ethical point of view. Political economists grow very learned and even fascinating over the wages question, but usually on entirely economical grounds ; while the just distribution of profits can best be discussed upon grounds covering both economics and ethics, for justice and equity are involved in the consideration of the subject.

A just distribution of profits, by which support and provision for old age may be secured, depends much more upon the cost of living, habits of frugality, temperance, good morals, sanitary conditions, educational privileges, and various forces of a moral nature, than upon purely economical conditions. We must therefore view the whole superstructure in looking at the labor question, and not merely the economical shingles of the edifice.

If I were speaking from the pulpit, and wished to

frame a compound subject from language taken from Scripture, I should say, whatsover ye sow, that also shall ye reap, and he that is faithful over a few things shall be made ruler over many. At least, the principles underlying the sayings from which such a subject would be drawn apply most forcibly to the consideration of the relations of employers and employed, and of each to society.

In this spirit I shall deal with the topic I have selected, — the relation of political economy to the labor question.

During the past one hundred years, political economy, as a separate branch of philosophy, has sprung into existence. The age has been one of material progress. Economics have ruled almost at the expense of ethics, although the same age has seen wonderful structures of charitable and educational design grow into existence. The strides civilization has made command our admiration, and its onward steps are marked by numerous and convincing evidences; but such evidences are outside the science of political economy, and are only considered by it as the cost may enter into the distribution of wealth it seeks to create, but not as means for a happier and better condition wherein wealth could be more successfully produced.

Material progress has surpassed that of the arts, painting and sculpture, and literature, for they live as well in the past ; and present efforts are rather to approach and equal, than to excel, the productions of old.

Under the spur of this progress political economy has flourished, — first, by the patronage and through the admiration of all classes. England gave it birth, and to it her writers claim she owes her industrial position in the past. It may be that to a too blind following of later teachings she owes, to-day, the partial loss of her old industrial supremacy. I am not speaking of the Manchester school as such, but of the whole orthodox school of economists, which never admits to its curriculum the study of conditions not purely economical. America, if she desires to occupy the place England is vacating, must take lessons of her mother, and profit by her mistakes.

The old school has been content to teach the laws |
that regulate the production, distribution, and exchange
of wealth ; and these laws have formed the whole of
the science of political economy, so far as it can be
called a science. It has studiously avoided all other
matters, and, in the endeavors of its devotees to con-
stitute it a science, has taken no cognizance of the
conditions which, favorable or unfavorable, must attend
the participators in the production, distribution, and
exchange of commodities. It has been content to
limit itself to things and their relations to individual
and national wealth, more particularly the latter, rather
than to include in its sphere of creed the vital relations
of men. Even Mr. Mill, perhaps the most brilliant
writer of the age upon the topic we are considering,
informs us [1] that " political economy is concerned with
man solely as a being who desires to possess wealth,
and who is capable of judging of the comparative
efficacy of means to that end. It makes entire abstraction of every other human passion or motive,
except those which may be regarded as perpetually

[1] Essays on Some Unpublished Questions, 1844.

antagonizing principles to the desire of wealth ; namely, aversion to labor, and desire of the present enjoyment of costly indulgences. . . . Political economy considers mankind as occupied solely in acquiring and consuming wealth." Professor John K. Ingram [1] calls this a vicious abstraction, which meets us on the very threshold of political economy ; and Professor F. A. Walker,[2] commenting upon this saying of Mill's, remarks, " If Mr. Mill had merely meant that the political economist should begin by inquiring what such a monstrous race would do under the impulse of the antagonizing forces of greed and indolence, no one could have taken exception. But Mr. Mill did not mean this. He meant that the political economist should end here ; should literally make entire abstraction, once for all, of every other human passion or motive ; and at no point in his reasoning should take account of any one of a score of recognizable and appreciable motives and feelings which enter to influence the actions of men in respect to wealth, love of

[1] Penn Monthly, November, 1879.

[2] In Sunday Afternoon, May, 1879.

country, love of home, love of friends, mutual sympathy among members of the same class; respect for labor, and interest in the laboring class, on the part of the community at large; good will between landlord and tenant, between employer and employed; the power of custom and tradition; the force of inertia, ignorance, and superstition."

Mr. Mill's statements represent the tenets of the old school, although the founder of the science, Adam Smith, began his labors in it as a professor of moral philosophy, and taught it as a branch of that philosophy. His followers, in their ambition, have strayed far from the doctrines of their great master; and, with their departure from him, political economy has lost the sympathy and even the attention of the wage-workers of English and American communities, the very support it largely needs and should have. But it would be unreasonable to expect them to have much reverence for what Carlyle has denominated "the dismal science," and George Howell "the grab-all science;" "for," says the latter, "its fundamental principles seem to be based on the Quaker's advice to his son, 'Make money honestly if you can, but make money.'" The majority of the followers of Smith have forgotten that Christianity says, "Thou shalt love thy neighbor as thyself;" "Do unto others as ye would that men should do unto you;" "Love one another;" "Bear ye one another's burdens." On the other hand, they practically say, Love thyself; seek thine own advantage ; promote thine own welfare ; put money in thy purse : the welfare of others is not thy business.

It is because of this hard, unsympathetic nature of the so-called science of political economy that the labor question has come to be considered as distinct from it, and because of the departure from sound ethical features of the science by most of the leading writers, there has sprung up, within a few years, a new school, which bids fair to include on its roll of pupils the men in all civilized lands who seek by legitimate means, and without revolution, the amelioration of unfavorable industrial and social relations wherever found as the surest road to comparatively permanent material prosperity.

This school is neither large nor powerful. Its first note came from an eminent Scotch divine, Dr. Thomas Chalmers, in 1832, who undertook, as part of his duty in a course of theological lectures to divinity students in the University of Edinburgh, to treat of political economy, which he defines as aiming "at the diffusion of sufficiency and comfort throughout the mass of the population by a multiplication or enlargement of the outward means and materials of human enjoyment." [1] He further declared that his object would be gained if he could demonstrate, that even for the economic well-being of a people their moral and religious education was the first and greatest object of national policy, and that, while this is neglected, a government in its anxious and incessant labors for a well-conditioned state of the commonwealth would only flounder from one delusive shift or expedient to another, under the double misfortune of being held responsible for the prosperity of the land, and yet finding that to be an element helplessly and hopelessly beyond its control. That the theory of wealth had to be examined in con-

[1] Introduction to Chalmers's Political Economy, 1832.

nection with the theory of population was a truth Dr. Chalmers recognized with the political economists; but he believed the great resulting lesson of such examination to be the intimate alliance which obtains between the economical and the moral, inasmuch as the very best objects of the science could not by any possibility be realized but by dint of prudence and virtue among the laboring masses.

Could this spirit have been breathed through all the wonderful volumes on political economy which have been written both sides of the Atlantic, there would have been fewer works periodically published upon the causes of depressions, and upon remedies for labor difficulties.

The creed of the new school is finding its way into the hearts and the minds of men; and it has for its advocates some of the best thinkers in Europe, with a few contemporaries in this country, who are beginning to question the logic of their old masters. I am proud to sit at the feet of these new teachers, and to declare my allegiance to such doctrines, which are the need of the world to-day so far as economical questions are concerned. They recognize as fundamental elements of political economy the humanity of the world and its moral condition, because the best humanity is to be found where the best morality prevails. They recognize that it is by the labor of the people employed in various branches of industry that all ranks of the community, in every condition of life, annually subsist ; and that, by the produce of this labor alone, nations become powerful in proportion to the extent of the surplus which can be spared for the exigencies of state ; and that, by the increase or diminution of the produce of this labor, states, kingdoms, and empires flourish or decay.[1]

Had such principles formed a part only of the considerations of economists during the past fifty or seventy-five years, there would not now be heard the lamentations concerning the decline or unpopularity of the science which occasionally comes up from the old school, nor would the laboring masses be averse to consulting and profiting by the teachings of the masters of one of the most attractive departments of

---

[1] Cf. Colquohoun: Wealth, Power, and Resources of British Empire.

human knowledge. We have the testimony of Professor Bonamy Price of England that political economy is undergoing a crisis, and is passing through a revolution, both in the region of thought amongst its teachers and students, as well as in the great world, in the practical life of mankind. This revolution will result well for the happiness and welfare of our kind; for it will bring to their support, to their improvement, to their education, the best and most thoroughly digested thought of the first writers of the world. Of this thought they have long been robbed. This crisis will not take from political economy one jot or one tittle of the grand principles which make it, but will add to it those vitalizing elements which will make of it at once a science and a philosophy which will commend itself to the understanding of the very workers whose products serve to create the want of the science and the science itself. It will result in bringing into the science the treatment of the uses of wealth, as well as its accumulation, distribution, and exchange, and incite discussion upon the relations of labor and capital on an ethical basis ; combining with the old question the old school always asks, " Will it pay? " another and higher query, " Is it right? "

Political economy has failed to see that the highest industrial prosperity of nations has attended those periods most given to moral education and practices. History is full of lessons from which the new school will attempt to teach that the growth of a healthy, intelligent, and virtuous operative population is as much for the pecuniary interest of manufacturers themselves as for civilization ; that the decline of the morals of the factory means the decline of the nation ; and that the morals, the force, the higher welfare of the nation, depend upon the welfare of the working masses.

From these premises I predict that political economy will, in the near future, deal largely with the family, with wealth, with the state, as the three features of its doctrines, and not confine itself to wealth alone. Under family, it will take cognizance of the relations of the sexes, marriage and divorce, the position of woman, and the education and employment of children ; the latter forming the most vital element in the economic considerations of the scientists, as well

as inviting the ardent sympathies of the philanthro-
pists.   Under wealth, the old chapters will be revivified
in the light of moral discernment, relative to all the
delicate, but always reciprocal, relations of labor and
capital.   Under state, political ethics will be taught as
a direct means of securing the highest material and
social prosperity.   ⌣

These considerations in the future will be demanded
to answer the question constantly put, how labor may
be rendered more generally attractive and remunerative, without impairing the efficiency of capital, so
that all the workers of society may have their proper
share in the distribution of profits.   This I conceive
to be the true labor question of to-day in the limited
sense.   Of course it is not that of the socialists, nor
of many radical labor reformers who find themselves
on the verge of socialism, but have not the courage to
adopt its tenets; but it is the sober question of the
sober, industrious, and thrifty workingmen, and the
humane, large-hearted employers, of our country, —
two types of men I prefer to speak to, hoping thereby
to indirectly speak to the Shylocks of both orders;

for, while the capitalists have their unprincipled Shylocks in one capacity, the reformers have theirs in another. The labor question, as I have announced it, seeks no panacea. It recognizes the faults of our civilization as those belonging to development, not to inauguration. " And that there is not any one abuse or injustice prevailing in society by merely abolishing which the human race would pass out of suffering into happiness." [1] It recognizes the fallacy of attempting to win advantages by isolated attacks at some special point, and that, like Christianity, civilization and its wonderful movements, it must attack all along the line, and hence make itself felt in all progressive steps and attempts to reach a higher and better life. It reaches beyond the hackneyed statements of the old school, that the interests of labor and capital are one, but incorporates them with another, that they are reciprocal ; and while it freely admits that capital loans machinery and all the auxiliaries of production to the workingman, without which advance he could not labor, except at ruinous

[1] Chapters on Socialism: Mill.

processes, it wants capital to feel that it depends for
its vitality upon the ability of labor to accept the loan ;
that capital invested in the machinery or the plant is
dead matter until the operative vitalizes it with his
presence ; and it knows well, that, if either under-
takes to do as it chooses, it either falls or is obliged
to accept the most meagre results.   It demands
that each should consult the other if both are to be
active and productive ; and its advocates find that
in all communities where reciprocal interests prevail,
and a moral standard actuates both parties, the best
prosperity is sustained.   And, reaching farther than
individuals and beyond industrial success, it claims
that a broad catholicity in trade is essential to national
success, and must take the place of the grasping principles of the old school, which have been sufficiently
disastrous to both individuals and to nations.   These
demands, which seek to avoid adjustments by all and
every revolutionary means suggested by enthusiasts,
and which appear upon the surface at every recurrence
of industrial depression, are based upon ethical
grounds, and yet in them lie the elements of economical progress.

From these statements it will be seen how thoroughly essential it is that political economy should deal
with all the conditions of men, — their passions, crimes,
appetites ; and should teach them how to make their
passions subserve the highest interests of humanity,
instead of abusing them and making them devilish.

Political economy, when it has been brought to the
height of its grand mission, should, above all other
considerations, point out the causes which have oper-
ated in leading people to good or evil, to prosperity or
decline.   Investigation is bringing these causes to
light.   When political economy and history shall have
progressed in these directions sufficiently for general
history to become philosophical, the first places will
not be allotted, as now, in most of the works of our
classic authors, to conquerors, haughty governors who
enriched cities by ruining countries, and to pretended
heroes, who have been the seeming scourges of
humanity ; nor will the grand epochs of history be exclusively associated with such celebrities, but will be
dedicated to those great men, the memory of whom
has been too often neglected.   I mean those who have

loved peace, honored honest motives, strengthened rural life, favored good local government, given protection to smaller and struggling nations, and contributed without noise or ostentation to the development of public prosperity by the practice of the highest morality in commercial and political life.[1]

Corruption comes from two sources, the high and the low, but generally springs from the governing or superior classes. It sometimes derives its chief strength from persons connected with establishments for labor ; and in this case the evil may have been propagated either by the proprietors or the workmen : but, no matter in what way it originated, it has really but one leading cause, — the transgression of the moral law ; and with such transgression there always comes industrial decline. The prosecution of this line of thought leads to the fullest indorsement of Le Play, when he says that "the best expression of the moral law is the Decalogue. . . . The people who show the most respect for these commandments are precisely those who enjoy, in the highest degree, competence, stability,

[1] Cf. Le Play: Organization of Labor, pp. 66, 67.

and harmony. In carrying on the useful arts under the influences of these divine laws and precepts, the best organization of labor is everywhere effected, — that organization which, *par excellence*, may be called the customs of workshops." Dependence upon such precepts would carry the people of the world over periods of depression without an avalanche of solutions at every stage for depressions. Just at this time, when prosperity has opened all the factories in the land, and crowded all our wharves with produce, the danger is great; for moral decline is especially provoked by a kind of error, finding its support in the doctrine of uninterrupted and absolute progress, signalizing the coming of an indefinite era of prosperity, for which the people are to depend upon blind destiny, without being called upon to merit it by devotion, personal sacrifice, or patriotism. This tendency, always a positive evil, is showing its influence at this time in suddenly inflated prices of commodities, a spirit of speculation, and a willingness to extend credits. The result can easily be foreseen in the light of the political economy of the labor question, — a few years of remarkable prosperity, and then a period of depression, when everybody will be trying to discover the cause of the hard times, when, so far as history is reliable, the chief cause will be the same as it ever has been, — extended personal credits. Inflated commercial credits will always bring disaster.

The principles of ethico-political economy lie deeper down than the laws of rent, profits, supply and demand, cost of production, the wages-fund, and the like. The true matter is the essential constitution of human nature and the fundamental relations of man to natural and moral forces. Out of these are drawn the ultimate justification of economic laws.[1] Without them, and with a too persistent adhesion to absolutely economic laws, the effect upon the industries of the world has been discouraging, as instanced in England during the past few years, when, notwithstanding all the favor legislation throws upon arbitration, more strikes occurred than during any similar previous period. Ethical wisdom alone can remedy such things. This suggests that the precepts of the Decalogue can-

[1] Cf. Henry A. James : Communism in America, p. 47.

not be preserved by a people, except when each generation has the power, and the desire which gives the power, to teach them to the one which follows; and this can only be secured by strong moral elements united with the sacredness of the family. In the sacredness of the family is found the strength of a people. The desire to see a family growing up begets the industry and frugality which allows of its support; and any industrial condition which prevents the young men from becoming the heads of families is in direct opposition to the best economical prosperity of the race. Statistics prove conclusively three things, — 1st, That, for the past decade, marriages have decreased in proportion to the increase of population; 2d, That divorces have increased; 3d, That illegitimate births have increased. These incontrovertible facts are either the results of definite causes, or the causes of results not yet made clear; and I contend that, in either case, society, and certainly the labor question, have the right to demand their recognition in the science of political economy, as directly affecting the equitable distribution of the profits of production and the condition of all engaged in the work of production.

The direct and sure bearing of the influences spring-
ing from a condition of debt cannot be over-estimated
so far as the evil effects upon industrial prosperity are
concerned; and when a family, in order to bring to
itself the ordinary necessaries of existence, is obliged
to find a margin against it at the close of the year, we
may be sure, whether the debt is the result of extrava-
gance, or want of work, or want of proper remunera-
tion, there is a lessening of moral tone and an increas-
ing carelessness of obligations incurred, results which
have an immediate and unmistakable bearing upon
the welfare of the community.   Surely, as a matter of
economics only, the grand science of Adam Smith
should recognize these things.

The influence of stable family life upon industrial
prosperity leads us very naturally to consider the position of woman in her relations to the productions of
a state.

The loss of proper respect to women always pre-
cedes decline of any description, and especially marks
the reign of immoral life.   That delicacy of sentiment
which, among Anglo-Saxons, shields women passing

alone through public ways, relying upon the protection of all men, when wanting, is too often replaced by gross impropriety, which excites scarcely any indignation even among respectable people. This loss of respect has been, in the history of the world, the result either of disorganization in private family life, or in the place of labor : but, however it grows, it always lessens resistance to corruption, — in fact, blinds the mind to corruption ; for it saps the authority of government to a greater degree than it does that of the father or the proprietor.

When woman is compelled by industrial customs to cease to consider the highest consecration of her life to be to the duties of maternity, she ceases to be the minister of the domestic circle, the very foundation of material prosperity. Nor does this consecration prevent her highest intellectual development, — in fact, it demands it, and her political power and equality too ; but when her wages and the wages of her little ones become necessary for the support of the family, that it may be kept intact, the natural result, in due time, is that very loss of respect I have counted so disastrous.

I have reference only to principles involved ; and these principles teach that the condition of inferiority into which people plunge when respect for woman is lost from any cause, whether from her work in a factory in England and America, or beside a mule in Belgium, or under a heavy burden in Italy, cannot be too much dwelt upon. The mischief it effects weighs upon society at large, and especially upon the wage-receivers, whom it renders too often incapable of satisfying that legitimate desire which prompts them to seek promotion in social ranks. In fact, whenever honest love has lost its attraction, and the consent of the bride implies a financial recompense, young men make no efforts to provide for marriage by securing a home for a family, but establish themselves prematurely, and roam about all their lives among boarding-houses, depriving themselves of the moral and material advantages intimately associated with an indissoluble union of the family and the fireside.[1]   Such a man does not, as a rule, hold himself bound to engage in any thing

[1] Some of these thoughts on the family are taken in part from Le Play: Organization of Labor, — a work I commend to all students of social economy.

which tends prospectively to moral amelioration ; and, having taken no pains to secure a home for a family, he has lost the very best opportunity of acquiring frugal habits. His family is compelled to give the preference to city factories, and, as a natural consequence of loss of respect, destitution and misery in time are sure to follow, especially when the combination with other manufactories, commercial crises, and public and private reverses have led to a stoppage of labor. Under such circumstances the establishment of wages becomes an embarrassing subject. Difficulties increase, leading to irritating discussions ; and the low moral tone of the operative, resulting from his first loss of respect for his wife, together with the grasping or impecunious state of his employer, brings about one of those unhappy conditions so recently observed in one of the cities of our own State. Not that other causes have not entered into this case, but those I have stated have been potent, and in themselves so forcibly affect the prosperity of communities, that they have their place in the philosophy of economics, where the political economist of the future will find them fully discussed.   In the home lies the future welfare of our country.

The material prosperity of a community depends much upon the health of its workers, and the health of workers depends in a very large degree upon sanitary surroundings.   It is that the physical condition of the people may be improved by every means social economy deals with the subjects of sewerage, tenement houses, light, and ventilation ; and in this respect social science teaches valuable lessons to political science.

In this connection I cannot refrain from weaving in a few thoughts from W. R. Greg, an English writer, with some of my own.   Dwelling upon the physical and moral development of the race as essential to prosperity, it may be asked, What may we not rationally hope for when the condition of the masses shall receive that concentrated and urgent attention which has hitherto been directed to furthering the interests of more favored ranks? what, when charity, which for centuries has been doing mischief, shall begin to do good? what, when the countless pulpits, that so far back as history can reach, have been preaching

Catholicism or Anglicanism, Presbyterianism or Calvinism, or other isms, shall set to work to preach Christianity at last? Do we ever even approach to a due estimate of the degree in which every stronghold of vice or folly overthrown, exposes, weakens, and undermines every other? of the extent to which every improvement, social, moral, or material, makes every other easier? of the countless ways in which physical reform reacts on intellectual and ethical progress and the prosperity of our industries? Under the constant teaching of a moral philosophy which shall embrace the political economy of the labor question, what a transformation — almost a transfiguration — will not spread over the condition of civilized communities, when, by a few generations, during which hygienic science and sense shall have been in the ascendant, the restored health of mankind shall have corrected the morbid exaggerations of our appetites; when, by insisting upon the healthy environment of our toiling masses, the more questionable instincts and passions, which, under such rule as I have indicated, shall have been less and less exercised and stimulated for cen-

turies perhaps, shall have faded into comparative
quiescence, and have come under the control of the
will; when, from the expulsion of vitiated air, disor-
dered constitutions, whether diseased, criminal, or de-
fective, which now spread and propagate so much
mischief, and incur so much useless expense to tax-
payers, shall have been largely eliminated; when
sounder systems of educating the young shall have
prevented the too early awakening of natural desires ;
when more rational, higher, and soberer notions of
what is needful and desirable in social life, a wiser
simplicity in living, and a more thorough conformity
to moral law shall have rendered the legitimate gratifi-
cation of our appetites more easy and beneficial, and
when that which is needed for a happy home shall
have become attainable by frugality, sobriety, and toil?
These conditions, so desirable to be reached, are not
impossible ones, and are not to be reached by the
revolutionary schemes of any party or sect, but by the
gradual adoption of sanitary laws in the dwellings and
homes of the people ; and the new school will teach
that the secondary, and often the primary, causes and

encouragements of intemperance are bad air and un-
wholesome food, which create a craving for drink;
bad company, which tempts it; undue facilities, which
conduce to it; squalid homes, which drive men forth
for cheerfulness; and the want of other comfortable
places of resort, which leaves no refuge but the publi-
can's parlor or den. And if, on the other hand, we
find that the consequences are poverty, squalid homes,
brutality, crime, and the transmission and perpetuation
of vitiated constitutions, who can say they cannot be
prevented by the sound administration of sanitary laws,
which shall prohibit the existence of bad air, of unven-
tilated dwellings, the undue multiplication and constant accessibility of gin and beer shops, and the
poisoning of wholesome food and drink? You cannot
discuss the labor question from either the ethical or
economical side without consideration of the temperance question; and from the results of such consideration it is perfectly clear to my own mind that the
solution of the temperance question is largely in the
control of the employers of labor. The interests of
capital as well as of labor, the interests of religion

itself, demand a sober and industrious community;
and, when the employers of labor shall demand absti-
nence from alcoholic drinks as a qualification for employment, the ugly problem, so far as the working
masses are concerned, will be far on the way to settlement. What will bring the employers to the same
issue is perhaps a knottier problem. The presence
of crime works a direct injury upon the welfare of the
workingman in many ways. It costs him more to live
because of it; it disturbs his sense of justice because
the convict works at the same occupation which furnishes his support: but, while the labor reformer
cries for the abolition of convict labor, the political
economy of the labor question cries for the reduction
of the number of criminals by the prevention of crime
as the surest and most permanent remedy for whatever
evils may grow out of the practice of employing convicts in productive labor. We make criminals now;
for three-fourths of the crime committed is by young
men who are temporarily led astray, and the fact that
fifty per cent of all the convicts in the states prisons
of the United States are under twenty-six years of age

only confirms the estimate. These accidental criminals we make into positive convicts, to be fed upon the
production of men outside. We shall learn better
methods in the future civil state, in which wise and effective legislation, backed by adequate administration resulting from a sound public sentiment, which will not
hesitate to punish when necessary with that punish-
ment which is most dreaded by the offender, shall have
made all violation of law, all habitual crime, obviously,
inevitably, and instantly a losing game, and when the
distribution of wealth, and its use, shall receive both
from the statesman and the economist the same sedu-
lous attention which is now concentrated exclusively
upon its acquisition.[1]

The intelligent workingmen of this country do not
object to wealth, but to its misuse. They know that
luxury — I speak of enervating luxury — depopulates
the country, and annihilates by degrees the class of
husbandmen ; for indolence and avidity tempt them
to quit a laborious occupation for one which is more
lucrative, though less certain. The ease in which the

[1] Professor F. A. Walker.

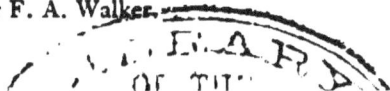

artificers of luxury live seduces the indigent peasantry, draws them to the manufacturing centres, and the country is deserted. Luxury corrupts the morals of men, — a truth no ethical writer will decline to adopt ; but morals may subsist with wealth : it is luxury which vitiates. It occasions continual variations of taste and manners. The expense luxury requires inflames cupidity ; money is run after, and purchased at any rate ; and from the moment this mercenary greediness possesses the mass of the nation, as it did to considerable extent in 1873, virtue becomes ridiculous ; honor, a chimera ; and the credit system takes the place of a sound basis for commercial transactions. Merit is then weighed by gold : dignities and employments and offices are valued only in proportion to the money they bring in. The rigor of law yields to the impulse of luxury. In this condition a fatal calm exists as a sure corollary, which looks like prosperity, but which simply forebodes a violent storm.

The ethical view of the matter insists that luxury debases the soul and the mind, and therefore demands that political economy should teach the science of the use of wealth, as well as of its acquisition; and the best use of wealth can only follow the possession of high moral character by its owner.

The use of accumulation beyond the actual needs of industry involves, of course, the highest elements of character in both the parties to its growth: for the resources which render organized or individual labor most effective are on the side of capital, while the industry, patience, skill, and discipline which give life and action to the dead masses of capital, are on the side of labor; and, in any community where there is no combination of the two forces, both will waste away, and the nation decline and perish; and unless there be an intelligent settlement, upon high moral grounds, of the respective claims of each force in the combination, ceaseless strife and conflicts will, by a longer and more miserable route, lead to the same catastrophe.[1] These propositions must be true if we recognize what labor truly is. John Ruskin has given the best definition: "Labor is the contest of the life of man with an opposite; the term 'life' including

[1] Anon.

his intellect, soul, and physical power, contending with question, difficulty, trial, or material force.   Labor is of a higher or lower order as it includes more or fewer of the elements of life ; and labor of good quality, in any kind, includes always as much intellect and feeling as will fully and harmoniously regulate the physical force." [1]   With this idea of labor, that man is richest, who, having perfected the functions of his own life to the utmost, has also the widest influence, both personal and by means of his accumulated wealth, over the lives of others ; and, again, that nation is the richest which nourishes the greatest number of noble and happy human beings.[2]   All this may seem to be strange political economy ; but it is of that nature which the future will demand as leading most directly to national and material prosperity.   The new school will recognize all the good that comes from the doctrine of *laissez faire*, or the "let alone" theory of the old : but it will insist upon the liveliest activity on the part of capitalists to see to it that their employés are put upon the best possible footing as to all the

---

[1] Unto This Last.   [2] Cf. *Ibid.*

material surroundings of life ; that they have all the advantages to health, morals, and happiness, which come from sanitary regulations and practical education ; and it will teach employers that a larger dividend can be drawn from the products of a community comparatively free from crime, intemperance, poverty, and vice of all kinds, than from one where these things are tolerated ; and it will teach labor to demand of society the conditions I have described as the surest means of raising wages, shortening hours, and giving it the most attractive and remunerative employment.

Laissez faire can never be a substitute for the higher principles of Christianity, and they always demand action. "Society, when at times it awakens, by periods of industrial distress, from dreams of a new golden age, to be realized by mechanical inventions, march of intellect, accumulation of capital, or by sound political economy, finds itself compelled by terrible necessity to abandon the system of *laissez faire*, and obliged to embark in a struggle for life, with the elements of disorganization and ruin."

The only effectual method of action is that in which

each person begins by improving and reforming himself; that is, a revival of feelings of duty and moral obligation, whose decay is always the primary source of evil, leads to innumerable individual efforts, and to an improved state of public opinion, without which legislation can do but little. To be sure, we believe that time will show, and the Providence which rules the destinies of nations will bring about its appointed ends by its appointed means ; but it is no less certain that each one of us, laborer or capitalist, has duties to perform, the responsibility of which cannot be shifted to the shoulders of Fate, — another and older name for the system of *laissez faire.* The new school will demand that every one who, in his public or private capacity, can do any thing to relieve misery, to combat evil, to assert right, to redress wrong, shall do it with his whole heart and soul.[1]

It will teach that government " should not connive at what is openly and notoriously immoral, even for revenue purposes ; nor will it permit, by its sanction, a free trade in vice, with only the restriction that it shall be carried on wholesale instead of at retail."

[1] Cf. Laing's Essays.

The very best results to be gained depend almost entirely upon systems of industrial organization with law and morality dominant in society. Comte has told the world that "the state of every part of the social whole at any time is intimately connected with the contemporaneous state of all others. Religious belief, philosophy, science, the fine arts, commerce, navigation, government, all are in close mutual dependence on one another, insomuch that, when any considerable change takes place in one, we may know that a parallel change in all the others has preceded or will follow it."

Every accession to "man's empire over nature" may be, and probably is, productive of good to mankind at large; but we should never forget that any increase in the material forces at our disposal involves an increase of intellectual and moral energy. Such doctrine will inspire all classes with an endeavor to remedy the defects of the present edifice, rather than attempt a new construction upon its ruins. Such endeavors may meet with failure in one age, and be followed by success in another, as grand mechanical

projects, instituted before their time, fail in the generation which saw their inception, yet become the admired
achievements of the next.   If the principle be true,
let it be followed by employers and by men till the
requisite higher notions of morality be planted firmly.
We can then join the passionate vehemence of Carlyle in this utterance : "The leaders of industry, if
industry is ever to be led, are virtually the captains of
the world.   If there be no nobleness in them, there
will never be an aristocracy more."

The political economy of the coming generation of
writers will insist upon proper contracts respecting
labor ; and, while it will throw aside the idea of productive co-operation, it will be able to discover a
system of contract which shall improve the whole
condition of the employé so far as his relations to
capital and the management of capital are concerned.
In the recent past, social philosophy has become more
and more cognizant of the distinctions between the exchange of commodities and the contract for services ;
and mildew will strike the political economy which
denies the validity of the distinction.   "Seventy-five

years ago scarcely a single law existed in any country of Europe for regulating the contract for services in the interest of the laboring classes. At the same time the contract for commodities was everywhere subject to minute and incessant regulation. . . . Can there be wonder that statesmen and the mass of the people entertain slight regard for political economy, whose professors refuse even to entertain consideration of the difference between services and commodities in exchange, and whose representatives in legislation have opposed almost every limitation upon the contract for labor as unnecessary and mischievous?" [1]

Political economy needs new life, a warmer blood, and a more thorough appreciation of the sinews of production; and, when this appreciation comes to it, or is forced upon it, the science will become a moral philosophy as well; and many of the dark places in the life of labor will be made bright and luminous with the light of prosperity.

The experience of England since the first years of the present century, when disorder in the sphere of

[1] F. A. Walker: Sunday Afternoon, May, 1879.

labor showed itself by unmistakable signs, furnishes
striking illustration of the absence of the principles I
am contending for. Orthodox political economy por-
trayed all the advantages of the division of labor, the
results of which are of the greatest importance to
mankind ; but, like all great steps in advance, it carried
certain evils with it, which could not have existed if
carried on in accord with high moral considerations.

The great proprietors of England did not take into
account the advantages the laborers once secured to
themselves by combining domestic industries with their
work in the manufactories. They, being exclusively
pre-occupied by the technical details of production,
forgot the duties which good morals would have imposed, but which political economy failed to teach.
The proprietors unscrupulously drew the workmen
from all rural employments by offers of tempting
wages, and, without giving them any guaranties of
security, and without giving the new impetus a moral
direction, they aggregated them in towns, and caused
the evil of the excess of manufacturing labor from
which the old country is suffering to-day far more

acutely than has America at any period of her history.

The English people, stimulated by the doctrines of a false political economy, placed too high an estimate upon the advantages to be derived from the accumulation of wealth, and at the same time gave themselves little inquietude in regard to the inconveniences and evils resulting from the sudden crowding of populations, subject to uneasiness, exposed to industrial instability, and impelled thereby to feelings of opposition irreconcilable with all social order. They did not perceive, nor did their economists teach, as they will in the future, that, by a continuance of evils resulting from the extension of a vicious system involving the inviolability of contracts between employer and employé, wealth must, sooner or later, cease to be a power, and the existence of the most solid industrial state history presents to us be compromised.[1] The seeming evils of this division of labor have been propagated both sides of the Atlantic by many writers, who, apparently ignorant of the truths history teaches as to the usages

[1] Cf. Organization of Labor: Le Play.

of prosperous places of labor, have persisted in a
systematic distinction between economical order and
moral order.   They have paid no regard to the reciprocal duties imposed by moral order upon employers
and upon workmen.   For example, they have assimi-
lated the social laws fixing the wages of workmen to
the economic laws which regulate the prices of goods
and products; and by this erroneous teaching they
have introduced a germ of disorganization into the
sphere of labor, and led proprietors everywhere in too
large a degree to hold themselves no longer bound by
conscience to regard the salutary obligations imposed
by moral order.[1]

Later writers will correct, and are correcting, these
false doctrines, but slowly, however.

In Mr. Herbert Spencer's recent work, "The Data
of Ethics," we are informed that "ethics comprehends
the laws of right living; and that, beyond the conduct
commonly approved or reprobated as right or wrong,
it includes all conduct which furthers or hinders, in
direct or indirect ways, the welfare of self or others;

[1] Organization of Labor: Le Play.

that justice, which formulates the range of conduct, and limitations to conduct hence arising, is at once the most important division of ethics; that it has to define the equitable relations among individuals who limit one another's spheres of action by co-existing, and who achieve their ends by co-operation; and that, beyond justice between man and man, justice between each man and the aggregate of men has to be dealt with by it."

These are sound propositions, taken by themselves, no moral philosopher can for a moment reject, nor should they be rejected by economists; for a moment's reflection upon their bearing shows conclusively that material prosperity is best subserved by their incorporation as chapters in the laws of trade, commerce, and production.

Are the principles I have endeavored to apply as belonging to the relations of political economy to the labor question the outgrowth of mere theory, or are they born of actual experiences, and do history and investigation teach their practicability?

History is bright with illustrations of the truth of the

propositions laid down, — even history back of the century of mechanical progress. The story of feudal wrongs is relieved by the grand life of St. Louis, who, in the thirteenth century, taught lessons of moral obligations which should exist between the lords and their followers, the employers of to-day might well imitate.

Forcible illustrations of prosperity resulting from moral influence and a public virtue could be drawn from the times of Louis XIII. (1610-43), while the decline of material prosperity as the practical resultant of immorality and profligacy became marked under Louis XIV. and Louis XV. (1661 and after). Later periods give frequent proof of the positions taken ; but I need not accumulate citations. I cannot, however, close without calling attention to the great progress which has taken place, and to some of the experiments which have been made in this direction. One of the most prominent experiments in the Old World was carried out under the direction of Robert Owen at New Lanark before he became imbued with socialism. At the period of his Lanark experience (1819), Owen gained respect and renown in distant lands, was sought by the great, was consulted by governments, and counted among his patrons princes of the blood in England, and more than one crowned head in Europe. The main cause of Owen's success began with the practical improvement of the working people under his superintendence as manager, and afterwards as owner of the cotton mills in New Lanark. He found himself surrounded by squalor and poverty, intemperance and crime, so common among the operatives of that day, and not quite unknown in our own. He determined to change the whole condition of affairs. He erected healthy dwellings with adjacent gardens, and let them at cost price to the people. He built stores where goods of proper quality might be purchased at whole sale prices, and thus removed the truck system. To avoid the enormous waste of separate cooking, he provided dining-halls where wholesome food might be obtained at reasonable prices. He established the first infant school in Great Britain; he excluded all under ten from the workshops, and made the physical and moral training of the young his special care. He adopted measures to put down drunkenness, and to encourage the savings of the people. The employés became attached to their employer, took a personal interest in the success of the business, labored ably and conscientiously, and so made the mills of New Lanark, in Scotland, a great financial success, as did our own Lowell those on the Merrimack a few years later. Mr. Griscom, an American traveller, visited Owen's mills in 1819, and concludes a report upon them as follows : " There is not, I apprehend, to be found in any part of the world a manufacturing village in which so much order, good government, tranquillity, and rational happiness prevail. It affords an eminent and instructive example of the good that may be effected by well-directed efforts to promote the real comfort, and, I may add, the morality of the laboring classes."

" Thus, one of these romantic valleys of the Clyde, which have been invested with the charm of poetry by Sir Walter Scott, had also been rendered the scene of ' an earthly paradise,' from a social point of view, by Robert Owen. Kings and emperors came to visit the model settlement, and returned with the conviction

that the elevation of the masses depends on the ready
earnestness and self-denying sympathy of those who
try to improve them." [1]

Sam'l Laing, an eminent traveller and social economist, writing, in 1842, of the evils of the factory system of Great Britain, and quoting Chevalier, the French
economist, who wrote from personal inspection, says,
" Fortunately there is evidence to show that these are
not necessary evils, and that, if a due regard be paid
by those concerned to moral obligations, the factory
system may be made to work well. The instance of
the American factories at Lowell, in the State of Mas-
sachusetts, is decisive on this point." And, after de-
scribing the Lowell system, he asks, "Why is it not
universal? Because," he answers, " certain *moral* elements of the American system are wanting in the
English. . . . Instead of leaving things to shift for
themselves, public opinion and a sense of duty have
made the employers of labor [at Lowell] responsible
for the moral superintendence of those belonging to
their establishments." These conditions, he further

[1] Kaufmann.

remarks, "should make us pause before we set down the Americans as a nation of inveterate dollar-hunters. In no country have the claims of morality and humanity been so remorselessly sacrificed to the right of property as in England."[1] And he might have added, in no country has there been such blind following of a false notion which excludes moral considerations from the science of political economy.

The experience of the Briggs Brothers at their colliery in England, of the Cheney Brothers at South Manchester, Conn., of the Fairbanks Company in Vermont, of hundreds of others who have recognized the great fact of the Decalogue, testifies to the soundness of the doctrines which will be taught by the economists of the future. When they are taught, and political economy is re-united with moral philosophy (from which it was divorced while a bride), we shall find the heartiest support given to the science by the producers of society in whatever walk their lives may fall. Periods of depression, which formerly, in ages past, used to alternate with periods of pros-

[1] Laing's Notes of a Traveller, pp 81-82.

perity on long sweeps, compassing a century, have gradually been reduced in the swing to shorter and shorter durations, so that now the oscillations are distinguished by half decades of time. The growth of industrial ethics will continue to reduce the length of these periods, till we compass them within the year. This is one of the tangible steps in the progress of civilization; and no greater can be recorded, or one having more practical bearing upon the welfare and happiness of the people.

I have not been ambitious to promulgate these principles, or theories, if you choose, with an idea they were to cure existing difficulties, or prevent the recurrence of past evils, but simply to make a new application to the wants of the future industrial world of those principles which alone have been successful under like circumstances in the past; and they are in accord with the Decalogue, the surest platform for the labor question — which involves capitalists and laborers — to rest upon, and by which to insure success.

READING, MASS., Oct. 13, 1879.

www.ingramcontent.com/pod-product-compliance
Lightning Source LLC
Chambersburg PA
CBHW021642270326
41931CB00008B/1131